WEIRD MOMENTS IN SPORTS

BY BRUCE WEBER

SCHOLASTIC INC.
New York Toronto London Auckland Sydney

ISBN 0-590-41646-4

Copyright © 1975 by Scholastic Books, Inc. All rights reserved. Published by Scholastic Inc.

12 11 10 9 8 7 6 5 4 3 2 1   7 8 9/8 0 1 2/9
                                            01

Printed in the U.S.A.

Contents

To Mom and Dad, my first set of coaches.

TAKE ME OUT OF THE BALL GAME

Littlest Big Leaguer

Few of the fans at St. Louis' Sportsman's Park on Aug. 19, 1951, seemed to pay attention to the scorecard. The first listing on the St. Louis Browns' roster read: "⅛ Gaedel."

"Must be a mistake," thought the fans. "No player wears number ⅛."

A surprisingly large crowd of 18,000 was on hand for the doubleheader between the last-place Browns and the next-to-last Detroit Tigers.

The Tigers won the first game. Then the fireworks began. Detroit failed to score in the top half of the first inning of the second game. St. Louis came to bat. Centerfielder Frank Saucier was scheduled to lead off.

Suddenly, the most unlikely baseball player of all time stepped out of the Browns' dugout swinging a toy bat. He was 26 years old, stood only 3 feet, 7 inches, and weighed only 65 pounds. He was a midget.

The number on his back was ⅛. Then the public address announcer told the crowd: "For the Browns, batting for Saucier, number ⅛, Eddie Gaedel."

The crowd went wild. Home plate umpire Ed Hurley just went crazy. St. Louis manager Zack Taylor showed the umpire several papers which proved that Gaedel was an official member of the Browns' team.

When the uproar died down, Gaedel stepped into the batter's box, waggling his tiny bat. When he went into his crouch, his strike zone measured less than three inches. Still Tiger pitcher Bob Cain tried to get him out.

Cain's first delivery was a fastball. It sailed high over Gaedel's head. Detroit catcher Bob Swift sank to his knees and made a target for his pitcher. Again the pitch was much too high.

By this time Cain was laughing so hard he could barely pitch. He delivered ball three and ball four.

Gaedel moved quickly down to first as the photographers snapped away. Browns' outfielder Jim Delsing came in to run for him. Eddie Gaedel left the field to the cheers of the crowd.

It was only a publicity stunt. But it worked beyond anyone's wildest dreams. The midget's appearance created newspaper headlines all over the country.

But it was Eddie Gaedel's first and last game as a major-league player. Club owners, showing no sense of humor, quickly passed a rule banning the use of midgets.

Shortly Thereafter

Minneapolis' Central High School had its own version of Eddie Gaedel in the 1967 season. Central's top pinch-hitter was Ricky Raski. His season's batting average was .000, yet Ricky reached base safely every time he batted.

Ricky, you see, was only 39 inches tall — four inches shorter than Gaedel. Central's coaches measured his strike zone at 14½ inches (he stood straighter than Gaedel) and rival pitchers couldn't manage to find it. Ricky walked every time.

Matchless Pair

The St. Louis Cardinals of the early 1930's were known as the Gas House Gang. They were one of the most exciting teams ever to play the game. They combined tremendous hitting, great defense, and superb fielding into several National League pennants.

Along with all their other assets, the Cardinals also got super pitching, led by their great brother act, Dizzy and Daffy Dean.

Diz, whose real name was Jerome, was the better of the two, but Daffy (real name Paul) was no slouch either. They enjoyed their best day together on September 21, 1934, at Ebbets Field in Brooklyn.

Manager Frankie Frisch tapped Dizzy to pitch the first game of the doubleheader against the Dodgers. And he was merely great. He scattered two hits in leading the Cards to victory.

Daffy took over for the second contest. He was even better. He pitched a no-hitter.

When the game ended, the Cards joyfully pummeled Daffy. As he stood by his locker a crowd of newsmen gathered around him, asking him about his great feat. Then brother Dizzy pushed through the throng. Wearing a hurt expression, he asked his brother, "Why didn't you tell me you were going to pitch a no-hitter? I would have thrown one too!"

Force(out) Of Habit

Johnny Evers, middle man of the Chicago Cubs' double-play combo of Tinker-to-Evers-to-Chance, made the most important play of his life without his famous teammates. It helped win the 1908 National League pennant for the Cubs. And it made Fred Merkle one of the biggest goats in baseball history.

The Giants and Cubs were locked up with the Pirates in one of the tightest pennant races ever. On September 23, the Chicagoans were playing the third of four key games at New York's Polo Grounds. The score was tied 1-1 in the bottom of the ninth.

With two out and a runner on first, Merkle slashed a shot to deep center. Only a fine play by the Chicago centerfielder prevented the runner on first, Moose McCormick, from scoring. That brought up Al Bridwell, who promptly sent the overflow crowd into a frenzy with a line drive to center which sent the second-base umpire diving for cover.

McCormick scored easily. Merkle, seeing McCormick cross the plate, followed the custom of the day. He stopped halfway to second, then sprinted to the clubhouse because the game was over. But not legally.

Evers spotted the oversight, obtained a new ball — the other was lost in the onrushing crowd

— and stepped on second. He appealed to home-plate umpire Hank O'Day who ruled that Merkle was forced out, thus canceling the winning run.

The Giants protested, of course, but to no avail. The league office ruled that if the outcome of the game affected the pennant race, it would have to be replayed. It did — and it was — with the Cubs topping the Giants' ace, Christy Mathewson.

Merkle's oversight cost his team the pennant.

Twi-light, Twi-bright

After pitcher Billy Loes bobbled a grounder in a key World Series game, he explained to reporters that he "lost the ball in the sun." And everyone laughed.

But perhaps Loes wasn't kidding. Look what happened years later....

On September 7, 1973, a twilight game between the New York Mets and Montreal Expos was delayed 11 minutes because of sun! Seems that the sun, setting over the rim of Jarry Park, was shining directly in the eyes of the first baseman. And rather than risk injury, the umpires decided to call a temporary halt to the proceedings.

Owen's Omission

According to the lyrics of "Take Me Out to the Ball Game," it's "...three strikes, you're out." But not always — as the Brooklyn Dodgers found out during the 1941 World Series.

In the first of many Yankee-Dodger Series, the Yanks led two games to one as the teams faced off at Brooklyn's Ebbets Field. The Yankees jumped out to a 3-0 lead with a run in the first and two more in the fourth. But the Dodgers came up with two in the fourth and two more in the fifth for a 4-3 edge which they held into the ninth.

Relief pitcher Hugh Casey quickly retired the first two New York batters, bringing rightfielder Tommy Henrich to the plate. Casey, the losing pitcher in the third game, inched closer to victory by throwing two strikes past Henrich.

Then, with the count at 3-and-2, Casey fired a sharp, low-and-inside curve that fooled Henrich completely. The outfielder flailed wildly at the pitch — and missed. Strike three! Game four to Brooklyn! Series tied!

But the Dodgers' joy was short-lived. If Casey's pitch fooled Henrich, it completely befuddled catcher Mickey Owen. The ball glanced off the tip of his glove and rolled all the way back to the screen. Since the rules require the catcher to catch the third strike, Henrich took off for first. He made it easily.

The Yankees took advantage of the break and scored four runs for a 7-3 victory. They wrapped up the Series the following day.

Not until years later did Hugh Casey reveal that he crossed up the unfortunate Mickey Owen by throwing an illegal spitball on the fateful pitch to Henrich.

Can't Win 'Em All

The 1916 New York Giants were incredible. Early in the season they ran off a streak of 17 straight victories. Then they came back to register another string of 26 consecutive wins, a record that still stands.

How did the New Yorkers make out in the World Series? They didn't make it at all. Aside from the two streaks which produced 43 wins, the Giants' season record stood at 43-66. And their overall 86-66 mark left them in fourth place, eight games behind the pennant-winning Brooklyn Dodgers.

Bad Day

Perhaps the most famous triple play was the unassisted TP pulled off by Cleveland Indian second baseman Bill Wambsganss in the fifth game of the 1920 World Series against the

Brooklyn Dodgers. It's the only such play in Series annals and is talked about every year at Series time.

But what about the poor batter? Imagine the horror of making three outs with one quick swipe of the bat.

That's not the half of it. The batter was Dodger pitcher Clarence Mitchell and the previous time at bat, Mitchell grounded into a double play. Two swings, five outs. For Mitchell, the designated hitter came five decades too late.

Bowie, the Healer

The greatest medical feat of all time? Healing a sore shoulder — from 3,000 miles away. The doctor: baseball commissioner Bowie Kuhn.

During the second game of the 1973 World Series, Oakland A's reserve second baseman Mike Andrews committed two errors which enabled the New York Mets to win 10-7.

Oakland owner Charles O. Finley wanted to replace Andrews with a better fielder. But World Series rules permitted such changes only in extraordinary situations.

So Finley forced Andrews to sign a medical report which stated that the player's shoulder was injured.

But everyone protested the injustice — fans,

reporters, even the Oakland players. Commissioner Kuhn stepped in and ruled that Andrews should be returned to the Oakland roster — in effect, "healing" his ailing shoulder.

After an absence of one game, Andrews came back. When A's manager Dick Williams sent him to bat in the eighth inning of the fourth Series game, the capacity crowd at New York's Shea Stadium gave him a standing ovation.

But perhaps his shoulder was hurting. In his pinch-hitting appearance, Andrews could only manage a weak infield grounder.

Big Thumb

Baseball historians say that Kenesaw M. Landis was the sport's most powerful commissioner. He must have been. Once he even tossed a player out of a game.

In the seventh game of the 1934 World Series, the St. Louis Cardinals were in the process of routing the Detroit Tigers at Detroit.

During a two-run sixth inning which extended the Card lead to 9-0, Joe Medwick slashed a long shot to left center. The throw-in and Medwick arrived at third at the same time. Tiger third sacker Marv Owen tried to make the play, but Medwick bowled him over to assure his triple.

Owen bounced to his feet and began jawing at Medwick. It took several minutes for tempers to cool.

When Medwick went out to left field to begin the bottom of the sixth, the disappointed Tiger fans decided to direct their anger at him. They began pelting him with garbage, bottles, and anything else they could lay their hands on.

Medwick retreated to the dugout, whereupon Landis decided that Joe should stay under cover. He was replaced in left field.

The loss of one of their stars didn't bother the Cards. They went on to win 11-0.

The Babe

Roger Maris' 61-homer season and Hank Aaron's career-homer record have only slightly tainted the records of the immortal Babe Ruth. No one can ever downgrade the Babe's marks of 60 in a season and 714 lifetime.

Need proof? When Ruth smashed 60 home runs in 1927, no other *team* in major league history had ever hit that many in a season.

Never Too Late

Things were so bad for the Cleveland Blues (now the Indians) on May 23, 1901, that manager Jimmy McAleer didn't even bother sending up a pinch-hitter for the pitcher in the bottom of the ninth. Why not?

Well, the Senators were leading 13-5, the small crowd was heading for the exits, and there was always tomorrow.

As expected, pitcher Bill Hoffer struck out. Then rightfielder Ollie Pickering grounded out.

Washington pitcher Case Patten gave up a harmless single to right. But it didn't seem to matter. The Senators still led by eight runs.

Two more singles and a hit batsman scored one run and left the bases loaded. The fans stopped short in the exits.

A line-drive double to left scored two more runs, making the score 13-8. Wyatt Lee began warming up quickly in the Washington bullpen.

Another single brought in the ninth run — and relief pitcher Lee.

A walk reloaded the bases, bringing up pitcher Hoffer. This time manager McAleer called for a pinch-hitter. Naturally he smashed a double to left, scoring all three runners and cutting the margin to 13-12.

The fans went crazy and poured out onto the field. Only by threatening to forfeit the game could the umpire get them back into the stands.

Cleveland went right back to work with a single (which would have been a triple except that it hit some fans still lingering in center field). That tied the score at 13-13.

A passed ball moved the runner to second and a single to left on a hanging curve brought him home with the winning run. Cleveland's two-out, nine-run rally was enough to take a 14-13 victory.

It Ain't Right(field)

Ever hear of a double play with the right-fielder serving as the pivotman?

This whackiest of double plays occurred on June 9, 1973, in a game between the New York Mets and the Los Angeles Dodgers. Here's how it unfolded:

The Dodgers had Tom Paciorek on third and speedster Dave Lopes on first. Lopes edged away from the bag when suddenly Met pitcher Jon Matlack threw over and picked him off. With no other choice, Lopes took off for second. First baseman John Milner threw down to shortstop Jim Fregosi who chased Lopes back toward first. Fregosi returned the ball to Milner who sent Lopes back the other way and threw to second baseman Felix Millan. Millan threw back to Milner, again chasing Lopes toward second.

That's when rightfielder Rusty Staub got into the play. Milner tossed to Staub who tagged out Lopes near second. Just at that moment, Paciorek decided to sprint for home. Staub fired a strike to the plate, nailing the runner and completing the double play with the rightfielder as the middle man.

Lots of catchers have pulled off unassisted double plays. Most make them in the usual fashion — batter strikes out, giving catcher his first putout; catcher then tags out runner attempting to steal home to complete his unaided twin killing.

That's too easy for San Francisco Giant catcher Dave Rader. On April 18, 1973, the Giants' opponents, the Atlanta Braves, had Sonny Jackson on second and Johnny Oates on first.

The batter, pitcher Tom House, attempted to sacrifice but popped the ball up instead.

Rader sprang into action. Leaping out in front of the plate, he caught the pop-up for the first out, then, spotting Jackson near third base, raced to second ahead of the retreating runner to complete the unusual DP.

Painful Experience

No one would blame John Zanhiser if he never played baseball again.

Pitching for Penn State (Behrend, Pa., campus), he covered first base on the first play of the game. The runner stepped on his ankle and spiked him.

The game was delayed for 10 minutes as Zanhiser recovered.

On his next pitch, the batter smashed a liner back to the mound which hit John on his other

ankle. Another 10-minute time-out.

Later Zanhiser had to cover the plate on a close play. The runner slammed into him, knocking him halfway to the dugout.

That was enough. Zanhiser came out of the game and took a seat on the bench. Then a batter fouled a fastball off into the dugout. John jerked his head to get out of the way and banged his head against the concrete wall. Another knock-out.

The game? John was the losing pitcher as his club came out on the short end of a 26-3 score.

Long, Longer, Longest

Leftfielder Bob Taylor of the St. Petersburg Cardinals had a heckuva slump one night. He went 1-for-13 in a game against the Miami Marlins of the Florida State League and saw his batting average drop from .368 to .250.

One-for-13? Sure. Taylor lost his batting eye during the longest game in the history of organized baseball. St. Pete and Miami battled for 29 innings before the Marlins won out 4-3.

The six-hour, 59-minute affair broke the record of 27 innings set in 1965 in a game between Elmira and Springfield of the Eastern League. And two of the Miami players had also played in that marathon.

Actually the game was technically illegal. A league rule stated that no inning should begin after 12:50 A.M. The game didn't end until 2:29 A.M. But the umpire was unaware of the rule.

The Cincinnati Reds must have been impressed with the St. Pete manager. A few years later they asked him to take over their club. His name? Sparky Anderson.

Playing the Rebound

Former American League president Joe Cronin was one of the game's hardest hitters — even when he was hitting into a triple play!

Playing for Washington against Philadelphia, Cronin came to the plate with the bases loaded and no one out. He hit a rifle shot toward left that had "double" written all over it.

Unfortunately, third baseman Sammy Hale managed to deflect the ball — with his forehead — right to the shortstop. The latter grabbed the carom on the fly and whipped the ball around the infield to complete the triple killing.

There was a fourth out too. It was third baseman Hale. He was out cold.

Hat Trick

Magicians have pulled everything from hard-boiled eggs to rabbits out of their hats. But none ever matched the feat of Phoenix Giant outfielder Jim Rosario.

Playing against Albuquerque, Rosario dashed in for a sinking line drive, dove for a shoestring catch — and missed! In the process his cap flew off, his feet went out from under him, and he sprawled on the grass.

Rosario picked himself up and began searching for the ball. He couldn't find it. He searched everywhere, but the ball wasn't there.

As the Albuquerque batter roared around the bases, Rosario disgustedly picked up the cap. And what did he find underneath it? The ball, of course.

By the time Jim returned the elusive pill to the infield, the batter had a triple.

Bases Loaded

The Brooklyn Dodgers of the 1920's and '30's were known as the Daffiness Boys. Their players were probably the whackiest in the game's long history.

They saved their zaniest moment for a game against the Boston Braves in 1926. The Dodgers somehow managed to load the bases. Hank De-Berry was camped on third, the great Dazzy Vance was on second, and Chick Fewster was on first.

Up stepped the looniest Dodger of them all, Babe Herman. The Babe looked at one pitch, then cracked a line shot off the right-field fence.

DeBerry scored easily from third. Vance sprinted toward third, and Fewster toward second. Herman took off like Secretariat in the Kentucky Derby.

Vance rounded third, decided he couldn't score, and headed back to the bag — at the same time Fewster was chugging in from second. A split second later, Herman, running with his head down all the way, also slid into third.

When the dust cleared, there were the three Dodgers, head to head, each holding a corner of third base.

The Braves relayed the ball to their third

baseman who tagged all three runners — just to
be sure! Vance was safe. According to the rules,
he was entitled to the base. But both of his teammates were out. Herman, standing at third, had
singled into a double play.

In a story which has become legend, a cab-
driver was parked outside Brooklyn's Ebbets
Field a couple of weeks later when a fan jumped
into his taxi.

"How are the Dodgers doing?" asked the cab-
bie.

"Great!" replied the fan. "They're leading
and they've got three men on base."

"Yeah? Which base?"

Parental Prediction

The three-hour time difference between the east and west coasts has created problems of adjustment for players in every sport. But it has also provided some odd moments.

During the 1969 season, outfielder Ron Swoboda and his New York Met teammates were battling the Los Angeles Dodgers at Chavez Ravine. As the Friday night game wore on, the clock in the L.A. stadium neared 10 o'clock.

At the same time, back in New York, Cecilia Swoboda, Ron's wife, was busy delivering their first child. Young Chipper was born just before 1 A.M. on Saturday morning in New York.

The Dodgers utilized their giant scoreboard to relay the news to the new poppa. "Congratulations, Ron Swoboda," the message read. "Your new son was born tomorrow morning."

Misnomer

What's in a nickname? Take John Franklin Baker, better known as "Home Run" Baker.

One of baseball's immortal sluggers, right? Wrong. In his greatest season, 1913, Baker managed to swat only 12 homers.

Out to Lunch

When Ed Sudol and his umpiring crew returned to their dressing room between games of a doubleheader between the Mets and Giants on May 31, 1964, they discovered that their lunch hadn't been delivered.

No problem. Umpires are a tough breed. And a couple of foodless hours wouldn't hurt. Little did the foursome realize what lay ahead.

Twenty minutes later, Sudol put on his mask and set up behind the plate to call balls and strikes.

Seven hours later, he was still at it. It was 11 P.M. The first game had begun at 1 P.M. The umpires' breakfast was long since a memory and the end wasn't in sight. Finally, at nearly 11:30 P.M., the Giants pushed across a couple of runs and took the second game 8-6 in 23 innings.

Baseball's longest day was over. When they finally sat down for dinner, the umpires ate well — very well!

Perfect Loser

Harvey Haddix was nearing the end of his career when he took the mound against the hard-hitting Milwaukee Braves on May 26, 1959. The little Pirate left-hander had been with several major-league clubs and was destined to become an outstanding pitching coach. But this night in Milwaukee was Harvey's moment to shine.

The Bucs failed to score in their half of the first inning. Then "The Kitten," as Haddix was called, took the mound and set the Braves down in order. He did the same in the second, third, fourth, and fifth. Then the crowd in County Stadium began to realize something special was happening.

Haddix continued his perfect pitching through the sixth, the seventh, the eighth, and the ninth. Twenty-seven Braves had come to the plate and 27 had been retired. It looked as though Haddix had pitched a perfect game, something no one had ever done in the National League.

But it had done him no good. While he was shutting out the Braves, his Pirate teammates had forgotten to get *him* any runs, either. With the score tied 0-0, the game continued.

Through the tenth, eleventh, and twelfth innings, Haddix was perfect. He had retired 36 straight Brave batters. Still the scoreless deadlock continued.

In the top of the thirteenth, the Pirates again went down without a score.

When Haddix returned to the mound, he was obviously tired.

The first Brave batter hit a grounder to first. But the throw to first was wide. The error cost

Haddix his perfect game. But there was still the matter of the no-hitter, the shutout, and the victory.

The runner on first was then sacrificed to second. One out.

The Pirates decided to walk the great Henry Aaron, putting runners on first and second with one out.

Up stepped Brave first baseman Joe Adcock, who owned a piece of the baseball record book himself. In one game, the Milwaukee slugger had powered four home runs.

Haddix peered in carefully for the sign and delivered. Adcock swung mightily and sent the ball rocketing toward the gap in left-center field. It rolled to the wall.

Adcock pulled into second base just as the winning run scored. Head down, Haddix walked slowly from the mound to a standing ovation from the Milwaukee fans. He had pitched the greatest game in baseball history — 12 perfect innings — and lost.

Triple Trouble

Before moving to Texas, where they became the Rangers, the Washington Senators played some of the worst baseball in the majors. If the Nats weren't in the cellar, they were always pretty close.

Sometimes, however, they did unbelievable things.

In a game in Cleveland on July 30, 1968, the Indians retired the Senators in the top half of the first. When Cleveland came to bat, they wasted no time. The leadoff hitter reached first safely. The next man got on too. Runners on first and second, no one out. Typical Washington situation.

Indian catcher Joe Azcue, the third batter, worked the count to 3-and-2. The next pitch sailed down the middle. Azcue swung and sent a screaming line drive out toward left-center field.

But Washington shortstop Ron Hansen was off in a flash. He leaped and speared the liner — retiring Azcue. He stepped on second to get one runner, then tagged the man coming from first for the third out. An unassisted triple play!

It's one of baseball's rarest plays. Prior to Hansen's feat, the last solo triple killing in the majors took place 41 years earlier, on May 31, 1927, when Johnny Neun of Detroit pulled one off.

And the one before that? Believe it or not, the Cubs' Jimmy Cooney made one only *one day before*, May 30, 1927!

Ruth-less

Yankee Stadium has always been known as "The House That Ruth Built." Its dimensions were perfectly tailored to the Bambino's home-run swing.

But in the 1926 World Series, the Stadium's construction haunted the Babe. There was a little open space between the grandstand and the bleachers which sportswriters called "The Bloody Angle."

In the second game, Tommy Thevenow, the St. Louis Cardinals' shortstop, smacked a hit right into the "Angle." Ruth charged over and searched frantically for the ball. He couldn't find it. Meanwhile Thevenow sprinted around the bases for an inside-the-park home run.

Luck Takes a Holiday

For the New York Giants, it was a very good year. So good, in fact, that they won the National League pennant.

But when the chips were down in the twelfth inning of the seventh and deciding game of the 1924 World Series against Washington, their luck finally ran out.

First, a Washington batter lifted an easy pop foul behind the plate. As Giant catcher Hank Gowdy reached for it, he got his foot tangled in his discarded mask. The ball fell safely, giving the batter a second chance. He responded with a double.

The next batter sent an easy grounder to shortstop. He bobbled it and all hands were safe.

The third batter slapped an easy grounder to

third baseman Freddie Lindstrom. As he bent down to pick it up, the ball struck a pebble and bounced over his head. The runner on second scored easily, sending the Series crown to Washington.

Easy Does It

Managers love relief pitchers who use good control to work their way out of terrible jams. But how about Nick Altrock, who won a game for the 1906 White Sox without delivering a single pitch?

Nick entered a game with the Sox trailing by one run in the ninth inning. The opponents had the bases loaded and two were out.

He took his position on the mound, received the signal from the catcher, then threw to first, picking off the runner.

Chicago then came to bat, scored two quick runs, and made Altrock the winning pitcher.

Long Walk

How can a pitcher walk a batter without ever throwing a pitch to him?

It really happened, in the 1973 season. Pittsburgh's Dock Ellis was struggling. When he threw two balls to Atlanta's Sonny Jackson, Buc manager Bill Virdon had enough. He strode to the mound and replaced right-hander Ellis with left-handed reliever Ramon Hernandez.

Braves' manager Eddie Matthews countered by sending up right-handed hitter Dick Dietz. Then Hernandez threw two balls to Dietz, sending him to first.

Baseball's scoring rules say that the pitcher who delivers the first two balls is responsible for the walk. But the hitter who receives the last two balls is credited with the walk.

As a result, Ellis was charged with walking Dietz — even though he never faced him.

Swap to Nowhere

As the 1960 American League season reached its midpoint, it was apparent that the Cleveland Indians, under manager Joe Gordon, and the Detroit Tigers, under manager Jimmy Dykes, were going nowhere.

The Indians had won only 49 of 95 games and were a poor fourth. The Tigers were even worse off. They stood sixth in the eight-team league, with 44 wins and 52 losses.

Clearly it was time for a change. The teams couldn't trade all the players. So they did the next best thing. They traded the managers.

Overnight, Cleveland's Gordon took over at Detroit. And Detroit's Dykes became the Cleveland skipper.

How did the swap work out? Just as you'd expect. Dykes steered the fourth-place Indians to a fourth-place finish. And Gordon's sixth-place Tigers? They finished sixth.

Delayed Reaction

For Dodger relief ace Pete Richert, the 1973 season ended on a note of triumph. His 12th year in the big leagues was one of his best. And the veteran hurler received the Rookie-of-the-Year award.

The award was no mistake; it was just a little late. Pete actually earned the trophy 13 years earlier when he won 19 games for Atlanta of the Southern Association. And his 251 strikeouts in 225 innings was tops in the league.

No doubt about it — an award-winning performance. Unfortunately, the trophy was misplaced and didn't turn up until the league president decided to clean out his basement — 13 years later.

Back-Tracking

Led by their double-talking manager Casey Stengel, the early New York Mets set records for losing — and zany play.

One of the whackiest Mets was centerfielder Jim Piersall, who always entertained the fans with his antics on the field.

He reached his peak on June 23, 1963. Batting against the Philadelphia Phils, Piersall cracked the 100th home run of his major-league career.

Jim was so delighted that he began running backward to first base. As everyone in the park — including the Phillies — laughed, Piersall took the turn at first and began going backward toward second. He continued in that fashion until he had crossed the plate.

Major-league officials were upset at Piersall's action. So they quickly enacted a new rule, requiring a player to face the bases as he made his rounds.

The backward run was typical Jimmy Piersall — a major-league *last*!

FOOTBALL FOLLIES

Abe's Sneakers

When the New York football Giants won the 1934 National Football League championship, they had three heroes: passer Ed Danowski, kicker Ken Strong, and clubhouse attendant Abe Cohen.

Both Danowski and Strong had enjoyed great college careers in New York and both were outstanding pros. But Abe Cohen?

Here's what happened:

The Giants and Bears were meeting in only the second NFL championship game. The same two teams had played the previous year, with the Bears winning 23-21. Chicago went on to win all 13 regular-season games in 1934, including two victories over the Giants.

December 9 was unbelieveably cold, even by New York's usually frigid winter standards. But a record crowd of more than 35,000 braved the elements at the Polo Grounds.

The weather had turned the field into a solid sheet of ice. As the Giant players warmed up, they began slipping and sliding all over the gridiron. Their cleats couldn't penetrate the frozen turf.

Giant end Ray Flaherty remembered that his college team had once played in similar conditions and had switched to sneakers to develop better traction. "Why not the Giants?" he thought. He passed his suggestion on to coach Steve Owen. That's where Abe Cohen came in. Owen sent clubhouse attendant Cohen to Manhattan College to borrow as many pairs of basketball shoes as he could lay his hands on.

Cohen took off — and soon the Bears did too. Led by the immortal Bronko Nagurski, the Chicagoans jumped to a 10-3 lead at halftime. A field goal in the third quarter made it 13-3.

Then, with about 10 minutes remaining, Abe Cohen came bounding down the clubhouse steps and onto the field, loaded down with sneakers of all shapes and sizes.

As the Giant players swapped cleats for basketball shoes, the Bears seemed unconcerned. They'd kept New York out of the end zone all afternoon. And time was running out.

Then it happened. Danowski hit Ike Frankian with a 28-yard touchdown pass. Strong's extra point made it 13-10, Chicago.

The Giants got the ball back and Strong twisted and turned for 42 yards and another TD. Strong's kick made it 17-13, Giants.

The fired-up Giants stopped Nagurski on fourth down and, starting at midfield, drove for another score, Strong going over from the eight. Then Chicago's desperation first-down pass was intercepted, setting up still another Giant touchdown, this time by Danowski.

Ten minutes, 27 points. The unbeaten Bears were soundly beaten. The Giants were champions of pro football. And, at least for one day, Abe Cohen was the toast of the town.

Fifth-and-Goal

Except for the handful of pro playoff games which require overtime periods, most football games are decided in 60 minutes.

Not so the Dartmouth-Cornell game of November 16, 1940. When the teams left the field, the scoreboard read: Cornell 7, Dartmouth 3. Two days later, Dartmouth was a 3-0 winner.

Cornell entered the game with an 18-game winning streak and high national ranking. Dartmouth was 3-4 and going nowhere.

But the Dartmouth eleven picked this day to put it all together. With a minute remaining, the Big Green led 3-0 and needed to hold Cornell only once more to register a stunning upset.

Cornell wasn't ready to concede. They drove to a first down and goal-to-go on the six. Running back Mort Landsberg drove to the three.

Forty-five seconds to go. Second-and-goal. Walt Scholl drove over guard for two yards, down to the one.

Twenty seconds to go. Third-and-goal. Landsberg plunged into the line and was stopped just short of the end zone.

Cornell sent in a substitute but, according to the rules of the day, had to be penalized five yards for illegal delay.

Ten seconds to go. Fourth-and-goal from the six. Scholl passed toward the end zone but the ball was knocked down.

That's when the confusion began. Cornell was offside. Dartmouth, of course, would refuse the penalty and take the ball on the 20. Three seconds remained.

But in the chaos, Referee "Red" Friesell put the ball back on the six and signaled fourth down for Cornell.

Everyone in the stadium — fans, reporters, Dartmouth players — instantly spotted the error. But the ball, said the officials, still belonged to Cornell. The Dartmouth team protested loudly, but to no avail.

Given another chance, Cornell's Scholl again dropped back to pass and this time hit halfback Billy Murphy for the go-ahead score. The successful conversion gave Cornell a 7-3 victory as time ran out.

Two days later, Dartmouth was a 3-0 winner. Referee Friesell had spent the weekend reviewing game charts and films and quickly realized his error. He wrote to Asa Bushnell, commissioner of the Eastern Intercollegiate Athletic Association, explaining and apologizing for the goof. Cornell offered to give the victory to Dartmouth and Dartmouth gratefully accepted.

Too Long, Tulane

Memories of the Cornell-Dartmouth game were revived when Miami (Fla.) defeated Tulane 24-21 on October 14, 1972.

The films showed that the Hurricanes' winning 32-yard touchdown pass had come on an extra down with little more than one minute to play.

But Miami decided not to follow Cornell's earlier example. The Floridians felt that the error was made by the officials and that Tulane still had time to regain the lead. (Remember, Cornell's winning score came on the last play.) For those two reasons, Miami decided not to forfeit. Tulane still hasn't forgotten.

Short Story

The football world went into shock when Bobby Douglass, Chicago Bear quarterback, ran for four touchdowns against the Green Bay Packers on November 4, 1973. Imagine a QB running for four TD's!

Guess how many yards he chalked up on those four great TD runs? Exactly FIVE! Three of his "runs" covered one yard each. The fourth was twice as good — *two* yards!

Mistake All the Way

When the Cumberland College football players examined their 1916 schedule, they quickly spotted an error. Next to the date "Oct. 7," the schedule read: "At Georgia Tech."

How could little Cumberland play against coach John Heisman's powerful Engineers? What a mistake!

But it was no mistake. Somehow the mismatch had been arranged, a contract had been signed, and Tech had guaranteed Cumberland $500. The Cumberland players went to Atlanta.

There they ran into the most incredible offensive performance of all time.

Tech struck quickly. By the end of the first quarter, they led 63-0. That set a college record that has only been tied once — by Tech, in the second quarter. At halftime, the score was 126-0.

When Tech kicked off to Cumberland, the visitors usually fumbled or threw the ball away, setting up Engineer scores. So Cumberland decided to kick off to Tech. Five of their kicks were returned for 220 yards, a 44.0 average. Everything Cumberland did was wrong.

In the second half, Tech slowed down. They couldn't match their first-half scoring pace. Cumberland held them to 96 points. No one has ever come close to matching Tech's 222-0 victory.

Records were established by the bushelful: most touchdowns on interception returns (5), most touchdowns on punt returns (5), most extra points (30), most kickoff returns (32 by both teams), most yards on kickoff returns (428 by both teams), most yards on all kick returns (726). Tech scored 32 touchdowns: 19 rushing, one on a kickoff return, two on fumbles, five on interceptions, and five on punts. They scored every possible way — except via the forward pass!

The all-time mismatch has become a college football legend. So has the following story:

In the middle of the third quarter, with Tech ahead by more than 150 points, Cumberland's quarterback handed off to his halfback who promptly fumbled. The ball rolled free and landed right at the quarterback's feet. But, rather than pick it up, he stood and watched it until Tech recovered.

When he came to the sideline, his coach was practically in tears. "Why didn't you grab that ball?" he asked.

"Who, me?" said the shell-shocked quarterback. "I didn't drop it!"

New Math

The days of the dumb football player are over. The modern game is just too complicated. But the University of Kansas team's inability to count past 11 cost them the 1969 Orange Bowl.

The Jayhawks led Penn State 14-7 in the closing minutes of a bruising battle. But a long pass by State quarterback Chuck Burkhart put the Nittany Lions inside the Kansas two-yard line with just under a minute to play.

Kansas sent in its biggest players for a goal-line stand. They just had to keep Penn State out of their end zone.

It worked — for awhile. A run into the middle on first down was stopped on the one. An off-tackle run on second down was snuffed out for no gain.

On third down, quarterback Burkhart faked the ball to halfback Charlie Pittman and kept the ball. He went into the end zone untouched, bringing the Nittany Lions within one point, 14-13.

State coach Joe Paterno never hesitated. With only seconds remaining, he signaled for a two-point conversion. If the Lions made it, they'd win. If not, they'd lose.

Burkhart took the snap, rolled to his right, and fired the ball toward halfback Bob Campbell. At the last instant, a Kansas defensive lineman reached up and deflected the pass which fell harmlessly to the turf. The Kansas defenders raced toward their bench to celebrate their 14-13 victory.

But their joy was short-lived. There was a flag on the play. Umpire Foster Grose indicated that Kansas had used 12 men on defense instead of the allowable 11. Penn State would have another chance, this time from one and a half yards out.

This time the Nittany Lions didn't fail. Burkhart pitched out to Campbell who swept left end for the two points and the 15-14 victory.

After the game, Grose told reporters that his crucial call was routine. "I count the players on every play," he said.

In that case, Foster needed some math help

too. The game films revealed that Kansas' 12th man had entered the game along with the goalline defense and had stayed for *four* plays. Penn State had managed its touchdown against 12 Kansans.

Bench Strength

Who made the shortest 95-yard run in football history? It was Rice's great halfback, Dicky Moegle, and he ran only *53 yards*! Here's how it happened:

As Alabama prepared to meet Rice in the 1954 Cotton Bowl game, everyone on the squad knew they'd have to stop Moegle.

Alabama took an early 6-0 lead on the combined talents of running back Tommy Lewis and quarterback Bart Starr.

Then Moegle (pronounced MAY-gil) went to work. He raced 79 yards for a Rice TD. With the extra point, the Owls led 7-6.

'Bama came right back, quickly powering down the field to the Rice 5-yard line. But Starr fumbled and Rice recovered.

On the first play Rice again gave the ball to Moegle. The fleet back quickly sprinted to the outside and, thanks to perfect blocking, broke into the clear. He outran a couple of slower Alabama defenders and crossed the midfield stripe with nothing but yard lines in front of him.

Then, as he suddenly broke free, Moegle was down. In sheer desperation, Tommy Lewis had left the Alabama bench, taken one step onto the field, and tackled the Rice star. Lewis wasn't even wearing his helmet.

Quickly the officials huddled. The rules, they said, stated that if a runner was in the clear and was tackled by a non-player, he must be awarded a touchdown. So Dicky Moegle, who ran only 53 yards to the Alabama 42, was credited with a 95-yard touchdown run.

He scored another touchdown later in the game and was voted the game's most valuable player in Rice's 28-6 victory.

Tackling Dummy

Two powerful New Jersey high school teams, Brick Township and Montclair, were hooked up in a gridiron thriller on November 10, 1973. With 15 seconds to go, a Brick Township defensive back intercepted a pass and raced for the goal line — all by his lonesome. As he neared the Montclair sideline, a figure suddenly dashed out and tackled him!

Screaming. Hollering. Chaos. The officials quickly ran over to see what Montclair player had done this whacky thing. They looked down and did a double-take. It wasn't a player — it was a *coach!*

Tough Job

When Dan Devine left the University of Missouri to become coach of the Green Bay Packers, his fellow college coaches warned him that the NFL was the toughest league around.

It took only one game at Green Bay to make Devine a believer.

He was standing with his team, directing the defense, when the rival New York Giants ran a sweep toward the sideline. Suddenly New York guard Bob Hyland hurtled out of the pack and barreled into the rookie coach, breaking his leg.

As his team gathered around, Devine was placed on a stretcher and carried off the field.

Could anything be worse? Sure. The Giants came from behind to top the Packers 42-40.

Bowling Along

Every college football player dreams of playing in a post-season bowl game. There's the Rose Bowl, which annually draws more than 100,000 spectators in Pasadena, Calif. The Orange, Cotton, and Sugar Bowls always sell out the house in Miami, Dallas, and New Orleans. And there are a few others too.

The holiday season of 1946, on the other hand, produced a rash of contests. No fewer than 43 games dotted the post-season schedule — on three continents. Like these:

The Glass Bowl (Toledo, Ohio) — Toledo beat Bates. The Papoose Bowl (Oklahoma City, Okla.) — Cameron beat Coffeyville Junior College. The Pecan Bowl (Orange, S. C.) — South Carolina A&M downed Johnson C. Smith.

The Aloha Bowl took place in Honolulu, the Derby Bowl in Nashville, the Peach Bowl in Macon, Ga., and the Tobacco Bowl in Lexington, Ky.

Dallas hosted the Yam Bowl, Los Angeles the Angel Bowl, Jacksonville the Tropical Bowl, and Houston the Optimist Bowl.

Military teams squared off in the China Bowl (Shanghai, China), the Japan Bowl (Tokyo), and their own Rose, Orange, and Sugar Bowls in Augsburg, Heidelberg, and Nuremberg, Germany.

Mississippi College downed the University of Mexico at Mexico City's Orchid Bowl and a group of Army and Navy stars tied 7-7 in the Lily Bowl, played in Bermuda.

Elsewhere, everyone remembered the Alamo Bowl in San Antonio, Texas (though fewer than 4,000 spectators showed up). More than 12,000 were on hand for the Bamboo Bowl at Manila, the Philippines.

Georgia Tech won the Oil Bowl at Houston; Tennessee State took the Vulcan Bowl at Birmingham; and Hawaii edged Utah in Honolulu's Pineapple Bowl.

And, oh yes, Illinois scored a 45-14 victory over UCLA in the Rose Bowl.

Field Gold

If Notre Dame's 1973 football team had a weakness, it was in the place-kicking department. Midway through the season, kicker Bob Thomas had attempted 10 field goals and converted only two.

Then the undefeated Southern Cal Trojans moved into South Bend.

When Notre Dame's first drive stalled on the Southern Cal 15, Thomas stepped back to the 22-yard line and booted a 32-yard field goal.

The visitors took a 7-3 lead, and again Thomas booted a 32-yard field goal.

In the second half, Notre Dame led 20-14 and needed insurance points. Once again Thomas boomed a 32-yard field goal to close the books on the Trojans, 23-14.

Bob Thomas had found his spot. His three 32-yard field goals provided the Irish margin of victory.

High Flyer

Life in the National Football League can be tough. But it's no problem for punter Ron Widby. He had things tough enough as a college football and basketball player.

During one holiday period he scored 14 points to lead his Tennessee basketball team to a tournament victory on Friday night in Shreveport, La. He jumped onto a plane, flew to Houston, and punted six times for 43 yards as Tennessee's football team defeated Tulsa 27-6 in the Bluebonnet Bowl.

Back to the airport, back to Shreveport, and back to basketball went Widby. On Saturday night Ron scored 18 points, Tennessee defeated Centenary, and Widby was named the tournament's most valuable player.

Sound Off

With Maryland leading arch-rival Clemson 33-0 in 1964, Terp coach Tom Nugent and kicker Bernardo Bramson decided to rub some salt into the Tigers' wounds.

Instead of his normal place kick for an extra point, Bramson persuaded Nugent to let him drop-kick. This legal but rarely used kick utilizes no holder. The kicker drops the ball to the ground, then kicks it just as it bounces up. But the ball *must* hit the ground first.

Bramson lined up seven yards behind his center, took the snap, dropped the ball, and booted it squarely between the uprights. The home crowd roared.

But as the Maryland squad congratulated Bramson, they noticed a flag on the play. Referee Jack Vest signaled "illegal procedure" against the Terps, nullified the kick, and stepped off a five-yard penalty.

Then, using the regular place-kick, Bramson booted Maryland's 34th point.

The drop-kick — it was the first one attempted at Maryland in more than two decades — was the main topic of post-game conversation. When a newspaperman questioned referee Vest, he got one of the most unusual explanations ever offered for a penalty.

"As I remember it," said the ref, "a drop-kick is supposed to go 'plink-plunk.' This one went 'plunk-plink.' To me, that's illegal procedure."

Bus-ted

Major college and pro football teams are accustomed to traveling in luxury. They fly sleek jetliners. They stay in first-class hotels. They're fed like kings.

Lesser teams aren't as lucky. When Billy Joe was smashing rival linemen as a top pro fullback, he grew accustomed to luxury. As head coach at Cheyney (Pa.) State College, he learned to put up with less.

As he prepared to take his squad to play California (Pa.) State during the 1973 season, Joe found that the bus company had sent a 46-seat bus instead of the 52-seater he ordered. On the spot, he had to cut six men from the traveling squad.

Once underway, the bus caught fire. When the blaze was extinguished, the bus could no longer run. So the driver returned to the depot and grabbed another bus. After a two-hour delay, the squad was on its way again.

What next? More misadventures.

A few miles from the California State campus, the door on the new bus fell off.

When the tired squad finally took the field, they suffered 12 costly penalties and missed a field goal which enabled California State to win 3-0. It was California's first field goal in 35 years.

Error of Omission

California (Pa.) State College, the victors over Cheyney, didn't have an easy time either.

Several weeks later they journeyed across the state to battle Waynesburg.

They arrived without mishap, along with a large crowd and a couple of bands, on a beautiful day for a game.

Only one problem. No officials. Someone forgot to assign the men in the striped shirts.

The game was called off.

Ace Receiver

"If you want something done right, do it yourself!"

No one believed that old saying more than Norm Swan, who was the quarterback at Longmont (Colo.) High School in 1953.

In an early-season game against Aurora, Swan dropped back and tossed a bomb toward a teammate. That was Swan's mistake. The ball bounced off the receiver's shoulder and into the waiting arms of Aurora's Bob Greene.

Greene quickly started upfield, but as he reached the 40, he was hit by a horde of Longmont tacklers.

The ball popped up into the air. And who grabbed it? Quarterback Swan, that's who. Given a second chance, Norm raced 44 yards for a score!

Phantom Champs

If anyone tells you that he graduated from Plainfield Teachers, don't believe him! There is no such place. But for most of the 1941 college football season, this nonexistent school rolled along undefeated, untied, and barely scored upon.

Plainfield Teachers existed only in the minds of several stockbrokers at the Wall Street firm of Newburger, Loeb and Co. The New York newspapers carried the scores of hundreds of college games every Sunday. One more wouldn't hurt, reasoned the boys at the brokerage. And so dear old P. T. was born.

Led by Johnny Chung, the "Celestial Comet," Plainfield wiped out Scott, Chesterton, Winona, Randolph Tech, Ingersoll, and St. Joseph. Each week another broker phoned the result to three New York daily newspapers (the *Times*, the *Herald-Tribune*, and the *Post*) as well as the Associated Press. And each week the scores were printed — along with increasingly longer game reports. Later in the season a *Post* columnist devoted an entire article to the exploits of Chung, "the stellar Chinese halfback."

Suddenly, the gag was up. Somehow *Time Magazine* had learned of the hoax and decided to expose it immediately. The brokers attempted to talk *Time*'s editors out of printing it, but they failed.

And so Plainfield's "publicity director" was forced to announce that a tragedy had befallen his team. Most of the players, he said, had failed their midterm tests. "Among those thrown for a loss at exam time," he wrote, "was John Chung... who accounted for 69 of Plainfield's 117 points."

Time's timing was unfortunate. According to the boys at Newburger, Loeb, dear old P. T. would have beaten Appalachian Tech 20-2 and Harmony Teachers 40-27 to complete its unbeaten season.

A hoax? Sure. But it was great fun while it lasted.

After the Ball

With just 13 seconds to play in a Canadian Football League playoff game on November 12, 1973, Johnny Rodgers caught a pass in the Toronto Argonaut end zone to cement a Montreal Alouette victory. The former Heisman

Trophy winner blew his famed cool. He did a dance, jumped into the air, and flung the ball into the crowd.

The two teams then lined up for the extra point. Each man set up in position and waited...and waited...and waited for the official to put the ball down.

Embarrassing moment. There were no more footballs. So, for the first time in history, a championship game had to be called off because of no football!

Few-tility

When the New York Mets lost 120 games in their first season, not everyone laughed. The football fans at St. Paul's Poly in Virginia knew exactly what the Mets were going through.

Beginning in 1940, the Poly gridders lost 21 straight games before gaining a tie. Then, just when things began to look better, Poly proceeded to lose its next 41 in a row.

The streak covered 63 games and 14 seasons. And during one 22-game stretch, the Poly team was outscored 890-0, an average of 40.5-0 per game.

Even the Mets won one once in a while.

Wrong-Way Roy

Probably the most famous foul-up in sports history occurred in the 1929 Rose Bowl game. A capacity crowd of 70,000 gathered to watch the powerhouse of the East, Georgia Tech, take on the best in the West, California.

The experts rated the game a toss-up, and *The New York Times* correctly predicted that a break might decide the outcome.

The two teams battled evenly into the second quarter with neither side scoring. With Tech on its own 23-yard line, halfback Stumpy Thomason took off on a counter play. Thomason was hit hard. The ball popped into the air. California's veteran center and captain-elect Roy Riegels picked it off.

Riegels took a couple of steps toward the Tech goal line, then cut across the field, pursued by the entire Yellow Jacket team. At this point, Riegels lost his sense of direction and began heading for his own goal line. Players from both teams stood by in shock.

Quickly Cal's all-star halfback Benny Lom sized up the situation and took off after Riegels. But the faster Lom went, the faster Riegels went. Lom finally caught his teammate at the Cal 3-yard line and spun him around. But there to greet him was the entire Tech team. When the dust cleared, Cal had the ball on their own 1-yard line.

On first down, Lom attempted to punt out of the end zone but Vance Maree of Tech blocked the kick. The ball squirted out of the end zone. The officials awarded Georgia Tech a safety. They took a 2-0 lead.

Tech scored again in the third quarter, upping its lead to 8-0. A California touchdown closed the gap to 8-7 (there was no two-point conversion in 1929). But then time ran out.

Wrong-Way Roy Riegels' boner gave the Rose Bowl win to Tech and gave him a nickname he was never to lose.

U-Turn

Roy Riegels isn't the only football player to have run the wrong way. Unfortunately for him, his boo-boo was the costliest.

Snooks Dowd, a former major-league baseball player, once picked up a loose football and ran 70 yards the wrong way — toward his own goal line.

But Snooks caught his error in time, changed direction, and weaved his way back up the field for a touchdown. On the way to six points, Dowd covered more than 200 yards.

Marshall Plan

Pro football had its own version of Roy Riegels' wrong-way run. The unlucky player? Defensive end Jim Marshall of the Minnesota Vikings, who later became an all-pro.

His hour of gloom came in San Francisco's Kezar Stadium, Oct. 28, 1964. Forty-Niner quarterback George Mira dropped straight back and hit halfback Billy Kilmer on the San Francisco 40-yard line.

Two Vikings sandwiched Kilmer and popped the ball loose. Marshall scooped it up and sprinted for the goal line. Blessed with great speed, he quickly pulled away from his pursuers — perhaps quicker than he would have thought possible.

After 60 yards he jubilantly crossed the goal line and turned toward his bench. But the first person to congratulate him was the 49ers' Bruce Bosley. Marshall's wrong-way run had scored two points for San Francisco on a safety.

Totally embarrassed, Marshall left the field, head down. Fortunately his error wasn't as crucial as Roy Riegels'. The Vikings managed to hang on for a 27-22 win.

BASKETBALL'S HOOP-LA

Using His Head

John Stobel of North Andover (Mass.) High School raced downcourt ahead of the Wareham High defenders. He grabbed a long feed from a teammate, leaped high in the air, shot the ball, and landed hard, knocking himself unconscious.

Ten minutes later, Stobel regained consciousness and found that he had scored the game-winning basket!

Fair Share

Contact lenses are the greatest things to hit sports since sneakers — except when they're lost.

It's a common scene in basketball. A whistle blows, the players and officials plunge to their knees, and they begin sweeping the entire floor.

Sometimes the elusive lens is found. And sometimes it isn't.

Midway through the first quarter of an Indiana state tournament game, Frankton High School's Don Paddock lost one of his lenses. The usual search proved fruitless.

Don's outlook seemed blurry at best. Then Frankton cheerleader Kay Alexander came to his rescue.

She popped out one of her lenses and handed it to Don who immediately inserted it.

How did he do with the borrowed lens? He only hit nine of 22 from the field and led Frankton with 19 points.

No one knows if Kay ever got her lens back.

The Middle Eye

Tom Koehler of Ohio's Capital University was minding his own business when teammate Gary Walters fouled an Ohio Wesleyan opponent. The two came crashing into Koehler, dislodging one of his contact lenses.

Again everyone searched for it and again they failed. But in this case, with no cheerleader to help him, Koehler had to leave the game.

After the contest, as the teams showered, Walters was scratching around and found his teammate's missing lens — firmly imbedded in his navel.

Where's Loomis?

Jack Loomis wasn't the greatest player in Stanford basketball history. But for one week at least, he was the most talked about.

Loomis, a 6-10 substitute center, entered a game against the Air Force Academy late in the first half. Three minutes and 50 seconds later, Jack was through for the night. He had fouled out. Somehow he had managed to average one "no-no" every 46 seconds.

Guest Ref

Vermont coach Art Loche and assistant coach Doug Holmquist were scouting Middlebury, the Catamounts' next opponent, against Brandeis.

For some unexplained reason, the officials didn't show up. So Loche and Holmquist were asked to referee. Their good work brought them praise from the coaches of both teams and head-lines from newspapers around the country.

They must have done a super scouting job too. Vermont thrashed Middlebury 82-46.

Foul Play

Wilt Chamberlain could do almost anything on a basketball court. The big guy could shoot, rebound, block shots, pass off — everything, in fact, except shoot free throws. Wilt seemed to have a mental block on the foul line, no matter how hard he tried.

But who holds the record for most successful free throws in one game? That's right, Wilt Chamberlain. In a game against the Knicks on March 2, 1962, Wilt canned 28 charity throws in 32 attempts. He also hit 36 field goals for an all-time pro record 100 points in a single game. His Philadelphia Warriors won 169-147.

Time-and-a-Half

A regulation pro basketball game consists of four 12-minute quarters or 48 minutes. A hard-working pro is usually asked to give about 40 minutes of action.

But what about poor Wilt Chamberlain? In the 1961-62 season, the Stilt averaged 48.5 minutes per game, more than four quarters per start. He played nearly every minute of every game — including overtimes — played by his Philadelphia Warriors.

Prize Advice

One of the features of the annual NBA All-Star luncheon is the awarding of door prizes. At the 1966 luncheon, one of the prizes was a copy of Oscar Robertson's book, *Play Better Basketball*.

The winner? Wilt Chamberlain!

Bad Hop

In less than 15 years, Tom Gola achieved more than most people do in a lifetime: All-America at LaSalle College, all-pro with the Philadelphia Warriors and New York Knicks, head coach of an NCAA tournament team at LaSalle, and Pennsylvania state legislator.

But New York fans remember Tom best for a basket he scored on a shot he didn't take!

The Knicks had overcome all but two points of a 19-point Detroit Piston lead. But with about 30 seconds remaining, the Knicks' cause looked doomed.

An off-target pass at mid-court bounced toward the sideline. If the ball went out of bounds, Detroit would take over with a chance to run down the clock.

At the last moment Gola stabbed the ball and, in one motion, heaved it in the general direction of the basket. Amazingly it bounced a foot in front of the foul line, then skipped up — and through the hoop!

Gola's incredible field goal tied the game and the Knicks went on to win in overtime.

Bull's-Eye Bunny

Basketball buffs can argue for hours trying to decide the game's greatest passer, greatest rebounder, or greatest shooter.

From 15 feet out, there's no question about the last one. It's Bunny Levitt, whose free-throw shooting record may last forever.

Bunny, only 5-4, was (and is) a giant at the foul line. On April 6, 1935, he gave the greatest exhibition of foul shooting ever recorded. Entered in an AAU shooting contest in Chicago, Bunny stepped to the line at 8:30 P.M. with only one objective — to win first prize. He did much better.

The contest rules called for the players to make as many shots as possible before missing

two. Using a two-handed underhand shot, Levitt canned the first 499! Then, somehow, he missed. His first miss.

By now the clock had swung past midnight. Still Bunny shot...and shot...and shot. He made the next 372 in a row.

The clock reached 4 A.M. The remaining spectators cheered every shot. But the arena's janitors didn't. They turned off the lights. The "game" was over.

In seven and a half hours, Bunny Levitt took 872 foul shots and made 871. If the sweepers were true basketball fans, Bunny might still be shooting.

Heady Assist

In a game between St. Cloud (Minn.) Tech and Staples High School in 1955, St. Cloud's Tom McIntyre tried to zip a pass to teammate Larry Nelson.

Unfortunately, Nelson wasn't ready. McIntyre's pass hit him in the head — and bounced cleanly through the hoop! The winning basket? Not quite. Staples won by 12.

Rag-Tag Champs

Basketball has had its share of wonder teams.

First came the Passaic (N.J.) Wonder Five. Over six seasons, Passaic won 159 straight before losing a 1925 contest to Hackensack.

The Franklin (Ind.) High School wonder team in the early 1920's took three straight state championships, then enrolled as a unit — along with its coach — at Franklin College. And they continued to win.

But the most incredible squad ever came out of the hills of Kentucky to capture the country's imagination in 1928.

Carr Creek (Ky.) had an eight-man squad. And all of the boys were related to one another. They had no uniforms. And their home games were played on a rough outdoor court. But they certainly could play basketball.

They shocked everyone in Kentucky by reaching the state finals before they lost to Ashland High 13-11 in four overtimes.

Kentuckians were so excited that they raised money for uniforms and sent Carr Creek to the national championships at Chicago. The mountaineers didn't let them down. Quickly they knocked off Albuquerque, N.M., Austin, Tex., and Bristol, Conn. — all state champions.

They were the talk of the nation. Newspapers and wire services carried lengthy stories about the Carr Creek wonders. It meant nothing that they were eventually bumped from the tournament by Vienna, Ga. They had done more than anyone had hoped.

And who won the national championship? No one but Ashland, the same team which edged Carr Creek in the Kentucky state championships.

Three Sour Fans

The story of Carr Creek is only one of many in Kentucky basketball annals.

The 1952 state championship was won by Cuba High School. The community consisted of 200 residents, 197 of whom attended the final round. The other three? They lost a special draw and had to remain home to milk the cows!

Two-and-Two

During the 1965-66 season, Chris Kelley of Wyoming's Greybull High School pulled off an incredible four-point play — with neither team losing or benefiting.

Kelley came out of a scramble for the ball and, in his confusion, broke to the wrong basket. Just as he was preparing to lay the ball in, he was fouled by an opponent.

The goal was good (score two for the opponents), then Chris hit two free throws for Greybull.

Bad News is No News

When Princeton students picked up their copies of the school newspaper on February 26, 1965, they read that the late Winston Churchill had blamed former Princeton president Woodrow Wilson for prolonging World War I. And, to their dismay, they learned that Princeton All-America Bill Bradley had severely sprained his right ankle — on the eve of a big game with Cornell.

But Sir Winston had said no such thing. And Bradley led the Tigers to a smashing 107-84 victory over Cornell. On a sprained ankle? No way.

It turned out that the editors of Cornell's student newspaper had prepared a phony edition of the Princeton daily. They slipped onto the campus before dawn, removed all of the real copies of *The Princetonian*, and substituted their version. Except for the quality of the paper, no one could tell the difference.

All Through the Night

Which sports records will last the longest? Most baseball historians believe that Joe DiMaggio's 56-game hitting streak may live forever. In pro basketball, thanks to the invention of the 24-second clock, it's unlikely that there will ever be a longer game than the one played by the Indianapolis Olympians and Rochester Royals on Jan. 6, 1951.

Indianapolis raced off to a 20-10 first-quarter lead and the Royals spent the remaining three quarters battling back. By outscoring the Olympians 12-8 in the fourth period they managed to knot the score at 65-65.

Then the real battle began. Each team tallied two points in the first five-minute overtime, none in the second, two in the third, none in the fourth, and, in a scoring spree, four in the fifth.

Early in the sixth overtime the Royals got the ball and decided to hold it. After a late time-out, they ran a set play but it failed. In the scramble for the ball, Indianapolis' Alex Groza batted the ball out to Paul Walther who relayed downcourt to Ralph Beard. Beard's lay-up with one second to go gave the Olympians a 75-73 victory. Seventy-eight minutes after it started, pro basketball's longest game was over.

Endurance Test

When the players left the court they looked as though they'd been playing for six days. In fact, they had.

The exhausted athletes were basketball players from Butler High School (Vandalia, Ohio). They decided to raise money for their favorite charity by playing the world's longest basketball game. And 150 hours after they began, they had accomplished their goal.

During the lengthy outdoor contest, the boys played through thunderstorms and scorching heat which at times raised the temperature of the asphalt court up to 135 degrees. They slept in tents next to the courts and ate food brought by their parents. During the six days they consumed 750 pounds of ice and 270 gallons of liquid.

The Butler boys made the Rochester-Indianapolis six-overtimer in the pro's seem like child's play.

One Way to Win

Ever wonder why basketball players spend so much time practicing foul shooting? The folks in Jamaica, Iowa, have the answer.

In a game against Bayard High School, Jamaica tossed in 25 free throws — and won 25-16!

Fastest Break

Basketball players spend countless hours polishing their shooting. But it's unlikely that Bill Sharman, the Celtics' all-pro guard, ever worked on the shot he canned during the 1957 NBA All-Star game at Boston.

Playing for the East team, Sharman took a feed off a defensive rebound, whirled, and spotted Celtic teammate Bob Cousy breaking to the opposite basket.

As he'd done so many times, Sharman drew back and fired a court-length pass to Cousy. It was too high! About 10 feet too high. Cousy watched the ball sail over his head — and cleanly through the basket. Sharman had canned an 84-foot shot.

Blessed Memory

Over the years, Lehigh and Muhlenberg have established a great traditional college rivalry in eastern Pennsylvania.

During the 1966-67 season, Lehigh won the first basketball game between the two schools by 13 points, 73-60.

When the teams met again, Muhlenberg coach Ken Moyer tried to motivate his team by taping the word "Remember" to the front of their jerseys.

It worked. Muhlenberg remembered well. Too well, in fact. They again lost by 13.

Dog-matic

Basketball officials are accustomed to biting criticism. But not the kind referee Bill Fouts received during a Gonzaga-Idaho game.

Fouts had withstood all the verbal abuse the Gonzaga fans could dish out. Late in the game, he stood on the sideline in order to hand the ball to an Idaho player. Just then, Salty, Gonzaga's canine mascot, dashed out and took a bite out of Fouts' leg.

Fouts' bark was stronger than Salty's bite; Idaho won.

Smooth Finish

Basketball games have been called off for a variety of reasons — holes in the roof, water on the floor, etc.

Now try this one. A 1966 game between Dallas Baptist College and Tyler Junior College was postponed because the playing floor was too heavily waxed.

Roundball Roundtrip

Back in 1960, powerful Miller High School of Corpus Christi, Tex., drove nearly 150 miles to play rival Alamo Heights of San Antonio.

The Miller squad had barely begun stretching their travel-weary muscles when they discovered that the game was to be played *on their own court*! So back they went, retracing their long trip.

When they arrived back in Corpus Christi, they had nothing left. Alamo Heights romped, 68-47.

Quick Get-Away

Back when Jack Gardner was coaching at the University of Utah, the Redskins took on arch-rival Brigham Young with first place in the Sky-line Conference at stake.

Jack's club was in top form that night and ran the Cougars off the court, 82-63.

Coach Gardner was delighted. After congratulating his players, he jumped into his car and headed for home — leaving his wife standing in front of the gym!

GOLF GAFFS, TRACK TRICKS, AND OTHER LIGHT CLASSICS

Lunch Time

On his way to a fabulous summer of 1973, golfer Tom Weiskopf made more than his share of great shots. Chances are, though, that his most memorable hole was the ninth at the Oakmont (Pa.) Country Club during the final round of the U. S. Open tournament.

Through the early holes of the round, Weiskopf was involved in an all-out battle for the lead with Arnold Palmer and Julius Boros. In fact, as Weiskopf approached the ninth tee, the three were tied.

Tom's drive took him more than 240 yards down the ninth fairway of the par-five hole. Then he boldly tried to reach the green with his second shot. Unfortunately it sliced off to the right. The ball caromed off a vendor selling periscopes, bounded into a snack bar, skimmed past three spectators who were sitting on the counter, and stopped on a shelf next to three loaves of bread.

Since there were no tournament rules covering either bread or periscopes, the officials were asked to provide a special ruling. Meanwhile the spectators offered suggestions and, in one case, a hot dog for Weiskopf.

Finally the officials decided that the awning of the refreshment stand constituted an obstruction. They allowed Weiskopf to place his ball two club-lengths from the edge of the snack bar. This, however, put the ball in a puddle. So Tom was told to pick up the ball and drop it in a dry spot.

That completed, Weiskopf pitched the ball to the green, which was about 20 yards away. The ball landed five feet from the hole. Then Tom sank the putt which gave him an unbelieveable birdie 4.

Weiskopf went on to a one-under-par 70 for

the round and a third-place finish in the tournament, good for $13,000 — and a free hot dog!

When One Equals Three

The experts say the odds against a hole-in-one are 300,000-to-1. In 1967, Oklahoma State wrestling coach Myron Roderick beat the long odds with a perfect shot on the par-3, 152-yard, third hole at the Stillwater (Okla.) Country Club.

But Roderick actually had to settle for a par three on the hole. Seems that his first shot flew into a pond in front of the green. Following a two-stroke penalty for a lost ball, Roderick fired his rare ace.

Woody's Woods

New York City educator Woodrow Goldspinner had his once-in-a-lifetime hole-in-one on a Catskill Mountain resort golf course back in 1956. He didn't deserve it.

Goldspinner sliced his tee shot on the 180-yard hole. It flew off to the right, struck a tree, careened back into the fairway, and didn't stop rolling until it plopped into the cup.

Habit Forming

Charles Browning is probably thinking about moving the 17th hole at Waynesville (N. C.) Country Club to his backyard. On June 27, 1973, Browning played two rounds over the Waynesville course. In both rounds, he used the same club and the same ball. And each time he reached the 17th hole, he stroked a hole-in-one.

Lord Knows

Lord Stanley invested $48.67 in 1893 and gained everlasting fame. The Stanley Cup has become the target of every boy who ever laced on a pair of skates.

Unlike other valuable objects, the Cup has had more than its share of weird moments.

In Ottawa in 1905, it was kicked into the Rideau Canal.

In 1906, the Cup-winning Montreal Wanderer team left it in a photo studio. A cleaning woman found it and turned it into a flower pot.

The Montreal Canadiens left it on a street corner in 1924. And a Montreal fan swiped it from a Chicago trophy case in 1962.

In the early years, the Cup went to Canada's amateur champions. Everyone knows that the

Montreal Canadiens have won the trophy many times. But did you know that the Montreal Victorias won it four times, the Montreal Shamrocks twice, the Montreal Wanderers four times, and the Montreal Maroons twice? Before the Canadiens won their first title in 1915-16, the city of Montreal had already taken 13 Stanley Cup championships.

The Cup wasn't awarded at all in 1919. The Canadiens traveled to Seattle (Wash.) to meet the Pacific Coast Hockey League champions. But Seattle was hit by an epidemic of Spanish flu. Several players fell ill. When Montreal's Joe Hall died from the disease, the series was canceled.

The 1950 playoff finals matched the New York Rangers and the Detroit Red Wings. But not one game was played in New York. The circus was playing at Madison Square Garden, and the elephants, cyclists, and clowns seemed more important than the goalies, forwards, and defensemen. The Rangers elected to play the second and third games of the series at a neutral site — Toronto's Maple Leaf Gardens. The other games were played in Detroit.

The New Yorkers did as well as possible under the circumstances, carrying the Wings into a second overtime period in the seventh and final game before bowing 4-3.

The Rangers have made some progress since then. Now when the circus and Stanley Cup conflict, the circus steps aside.

Long Night's Journey

On March 24, 1936, the usual enormous crowd gathered at Montreal's Forum to witness the opening game of the Stanley Cup semi-finals. At exactly 8:34 P.M. the referee dropped the puck to start the game between the Montreal Maroons and the Detroit Red Wings.

The experts figured the game as a defensive battle. And the two clubs did everything possible to prove them correct.

The teams battled for three bruising periods without a score. The game continued into overtime. Try as they would, Detroit couldn't put the puck past Montreal goalie Lorne Chabot. And the Maroons were equally helpless against the net-minding of Detroit's Norm Smith.

On and on they went, period after period. The clock approached and passed midnight. The Maroons and Wings played five more full periods and the score remained tied 0-0.

The sixth overtime began just as the others ended. Then, with little less than four minutes to go, Detroit's Hec Kilrea fed Mud Bruneteau who slammed the puck into the Montreal cage. The two teams had played 176½ minutes, the equivalent of nearly three full games.

As the remaining fans filed out of the Forum, the clock read 2:55 A.M. The longest game in hockey history was over, almost six hours after it began.

Too Much Law

New York State boxing rules state that all decisions are made by the referee and two judges. Their verdicts are announced immediately after the bout.

But back in 1952, it took a third judge and nearly two months for a winner to be declared.

Middleweights Billy Graham of New York and Joey Giardello of Philadelphia pounded each other for 10 rounds at Madison Square Garden on Dec. 19, 1952. When all the votes were in, it became apparent that Giardello had won a split decision.

But New York State Athletic Commission chairman Bob Christenberry disagreed. He felt that the decision should go to Graham. As ring announcer Johnny Addie climbed through the ropes to announce the decision, Christenberry instructed him to say it was "unofficial." Then Christenberry changed the voting card of Judge Joe Angello to favor Graham.

Giardello was stunned. He immediately announced his plan to protest the change in New York State's Supreme Court.

It was in a courtroom, nearly two months later, that the third judge of the fight, New York Justice Bernard Botein, overruled Christenberry and awarded the decision to Giardello.

Wait a Second!

When junior welterweights Al Couture and Ralph Walton met at Lewiston, Me., Sept. 24, 1946, they had no problem with the decision.

As the opening bell sounded, Couture dashed into Walton's corner as he was adjusting his mouthpiece, and knocked him out with one punch.

Ten seconds later, the fight was over. The official time was 10½ seconds, probably the fastest knockout in history.

Reverse Gear

Bill "Bojangles" Robinson was probably the greatest tap dancer in history. You can still see him doing his thing on some of those late-night TV movies.

Bojangles was also the all-time champ in a certain running event — although you'll never find his name in a track record book. He could spot anybody — including the greatest runners in the world — 10 yards in a 100-yard race and still beat them. He *never lost a race* in his life. The event? *Running backwards!*

Trammell's Travail

Paul Trammell, a sprinter for Nathan Hale High School in Seattle, turned in his fastest time of 1967 in a meet against Shorecrest High. But Paul never made it onto the track.

As his leg of the 880-yard relay approached, Trammell stripped off his warm-up suit and prepared to take the baton. The crowd roared and Paul ran. Ran for cover, that is. In pulling off his warm-up suit, he'd pulled off his track shorts as well.

Nightmare Derby

Ralph Lowe had a dream. A bad dream. A few nights before the 1957 Kentucky Derby, Lowe dreamed that the jockey on his horse, Gallant Man, would misjudge the finish line, costing him the world's most famous race.

Then it happened. Disaster. Ralph Lowe's dream came true!

Before the start of the race, Lowe asked Gallant Man's trainer, Johnny Nerud, to tell jockey Willie Shoemaker of the nightmare. Nerud relayed the message. It didn't help.

When the nine-horse field broke from the gate on May 4, 1957, Shoemaker, even then one of America's top jockeys, took Gallant Man toward the rear.

Midway through the race, Federal Hill had the lead. Iron Liege, ridden by Shoemaker's archrival Bill Hartack, ranged up to take second. Gallant Man remained back in the pack.

At the head of the stretch, Iron Liege moved to the front. Gallant Man, on the outside, began passing horses — fifth, then fourth, then third.

When the horses reached the sixteenth pole — 110 yards from the finish — Gallant Man and Shoemaker drew up alongside Iron Liege and Hartack.

That's when it happened. Shoemaker stood up in his stirrups. He thought the sixteenth pole was the finish line. He thought the race was over. The enormous crowd gasped.

Shoemaker quickly realized his error and dropped back down into the saddle. But the damage had been done. Gallant Man's rhythm had been interrupted for only a split second, but that was all Iron Liege needed. Hartack took his mount across the finish line, a mere nose ahead of Gallant Man.

The track stewards conducted an inquiry. Shoemaker quickly admitted his misjudgment and was suspended for two weeks.

For Iron Liege and Hartack — who went on to win the national riding title in '57 — the Derby was a great triumph. But for Gallant Man, Shoemaker, and, especially, owner Ralph Lowe, it was a failure that racing fans would never forget. Lowe's nightmare had become a reality.

Over-Over-Overtime

High school soccer games involve two 30-minute halves. With clock stoppages and a half-time break, the games rarely last more than two hours.

But when Brighton High and Gates-Chili High met in the New York State sectional semi-finals, it took three days to determine the winner.

The game began on November 2, 1971. The teams played two standard halves and four five-minute overtimes. Result: a 0-0 tie.

They tried again the following day. This time Gates-Chili broke the ice with a first-half goal. Brighton came back to tie in the second half and both teams went scoreless in the four overtimes.

The two exhausted squads took November 4th off. But they went back to work on the 5th.

Gates-Chili scored first again. Then Brighton tallied three second-half goals and hung on to win 3-2. It took six halves and eight overtimes — three hours and 40 minutes of playing time — to decide a winner.

The grueling victory didn't hurt Brighton either. They came right back to win the title.

Quick Thinker

Big Mike Belling of San Francisco's Galileo High School had won his usual events, the shot-put and the discus. Then he found that the only pole vaulter entered had reported in sick.

So the enterprising Belling grabbed a pole and won the vault — at the incredible height of *four feet*!

Foreign Aid

The marathon race at the 1908 London Olympics was one of the oddest and most dramatic in history.

First, there was the matter of distance. England's King Edward VII asked the Olympic organizers to start the race at Windsor Castle. This would provide a special treat for the King's grandchildren.

The distance from the castle lawn to the finish line at London's White City Stadium was exactly 26 miles, 385 yards. And ever since, the marathon has always been contested at that distance.

Friday, July 13, dawned hot and quite humid, even for London. The usual large field was assembled for the marathon but it started to string out not long after the start of the race.

A trio of Englishmen took the early lead, but the hot weather took its toll on them and South Africa's Charles Hefferon raced to the front. His pace was so strong and brisk that there seemed little doubt that he would win.

Then, with slightly more than six miles to go, his pace slowed considerably. And with about four miles remaining, Little Dorando Pietri, a 22-year-old Italian candy-maker, flashed past Hefferon and into the lead. A little later, 19-year-old Johnny Hayes, America's youngest Olympian, rushed past Hefferon and into second place.

But Dorando seemed unbeatable. As he reached White City Stadium where the race would end, he led Hayes by nearly a half-mile — with only a quarter-mile to run. Dorando Pietri strode into the stadium to the lusty cheers of the crowd: "Dorando! Dorando! Dorando!"

Then disaster struck. First Dorando turned the wrong way on the track. It was clear that he was in trouble.

Meet officials formed a human barrier across the track and, somehow, the dazed Italian turned around and began moving in the proper direction.

But after a few steps he began to stagger. Four times he fell and four times he pulled himself up and staggered forward. Finally, fearing for his life, several officials helped him up and practically dragged him across the finish line. There a stretcher crew carried him off the field.

Moments later, Johnny Hayes, still apparently fresh, raced into the stadium. The young American dashed across the finish line and was told by teammates of the events that had taken place before his arrival. After a check of the rule book, the officials disqualified the unfortunate Dorando and awarded first place to Hayes.

Long-ing to Run

The Dorando Pietri-Johnny Hayes story touched off a marathon craze in the United

States. The two Olympians were paired off many times in U.S. exhibitions. But, more than that, marathons were run all over the country.

One, in fact, was conducted in Yonkers, N.Y., on Thanksgiving Day, 1908, the morning after a Pietri-Hayes run-off at Madison Square Garden.

One of the Yonkers competitors was 23-year-old Matthew Maloney, an Irishman living in New York. He watched Dorando beat Hayes at the Garden, then decided not only to compete the next morning, but to run to Yonkers as well.

Maloney, a pretty good distance runner, had never before attempted the 26-mile-plus marathon course. But he left the Garden, went home for a quick meal, got some sleep, and started for Yonkers.

On the way to the starting line, Maloney covered some 15 miles, running all the way. Then he stayed up with the marathon leaders for about 19 miles. At that point — what else? — he fainted.

Old Goalie

Modern hockey rules require each team to have two goalies in uniform at each game. But it wasn't always that way. Until recently, National Hockey League clubs carried only one goaltender. If he was injured, they had to scratch for a substitute — right on the spot!

That's what happened to the New York Rangers in the second game of the 1928 Stanley Cup finals. The New Yorkers, in only their second year of play, trailed the Montreal Maroons one game to none as the second game began at Montreal's Forum.

Early in the second period with the score tied 0-0, the Maroons' star forward, Nels Stewart, zipped in on Ranger goalie Lorne Chabot. He got off a low but rising shot that Chabot stopped the best way he could — with his head!

The goalie crumpled to the ice, bleeding profusely. Moments later he was on a stretcher, headed for the hospital.

That's when the Rangers' trouble began. Coach Lester Patrick quickly spotted the goaltender for Ottawa among the spectators at the game. But Montreal refused to allow the New Yorkers to use him.

What next? Someone half jokingly suggested that Patrick himself play in the goal. How ridiculous! Patrick was 45 years old. He hadn't played at all for several years. He had never played goalie as a professional.

Of course, he agreed to do it!

When the Rangers returned to the ice, there was white-haired Lester Patrick — the Silver Fox, they called him — wearing Chabot's bloodstained pads in front of the goal.

Somehow he managed to shut out the Maroons through the second period. But the score was still 0-0.

The Rangers began the third period by attacking furiously. Within a minute, Bill Cook split the Montreal defense and flipped the puck past the Maroon goaltender. The Rangers led 1-0.

But Montreal wouldn't give up. They attacked harder than ever. With barely five minutes to go, Nels Stewart finally skimmed the puck past Patrick to tie the score 1-1.

Sudden death! Patrick managed to keep the puck out of the net during the early minutes. Then the Rangers began to take charge. Finally the center, Frank Boucher, skated through the entire Montreal defense, zoomed in on goalie Clint Benedict, and sent a hard and low shot into a corner of the Montreal cage. The game was over! The Rangers, the 2-1 winners, carried their goalie-coach off the ice in triumph.

The Maroons came back to take the third game 2-0. But the fired-up Rangers captured the next two, 1-0 and 2-1, to take the best three-of-five series and the Cup.

Saddle Up

Baseball fans know all too well that a game doesn't end until there are three out in the ninth. The same thinking can also be applied to horse racing.

In a two-mile steeplechase race on December 29, 1945, a horse named Never Mind II started with the field, successfully hurdled the first three barriers, then decided he'd had enough. He refused to take the fourth jump.

His disappointed jockey gave up and returned Never Mind to the paddock. Suddenly he got word that every other horse in the race had fallen. Instantly he got Never Mind back onto the track, over the fourth hurdle, and through the remainder of the course. His winning time was 11:28, more than seven minutes slower than the usual time for the distance.

Handicapper's Delight

One of the functions of a racing secretary is to assign weights for handicap races. Ideally, the weight will somehow cause all of the horses to finish at precisely the same time — a dead heat. In reality, races rarely work out that way.

But the racing secretary at New York's Aqueduct Racetrack could have asked for a raise after the 1944 Carter Handicap. As the horses swung down the stretch, three of them — Brownie, Bossuet, and Wait a Bit — were running nose to nose. As they swept across the finish line, seven-eighths of a mile after they began, they were just as even as when they started. Even the photo-finish camera couldn't separate the trio.

A triple dead-heat! It was a handicapper's dream come true.

Pea Soup Hockey

Hockey players are a hardy breed. If they can walk, they can play. But other factors can keep them off the ice.

The Boston Bruins and Detroit Red Wings met at Boston on November 10, 1948. They played nine minutes before the game was called off and rescheduled for the following evening.

Why? A fog, which had somehow settled into the Boston arena, cut visibility, and softened the ice. For the players' safety, the game was postponed.

Overtime

Most everyone agrees that hockey's 78-game season is long enough. So pity poor Ross Lonsberry. In the 1971-72 campaign, the veteran left winger played in 82 NHL contests.

Ross began the season with the Los Angeles Kings and appeared in their first 50 games. Then on January 28, 1972, he was traded to the Philadelphia Flyers. The Flyers had played only 46 games at that point. They utilized the talents of the steady Lonsberry in each of their remaining 32 games.

His 50 King appearances and 32 Flyer games gave him a grand total of 82.

The Longest Mile

When track fans picked up their newspapers one morning in 1936, they blinked twice, then tossed their papers away. The reports stated that America's premier miler, Glenn Cunningham, had won the mile event at New York's Knights of Columbus Games in 4:46.4.

"Ridiculous!" scoffed the track nuts. And so it seemed. The Madison Square Garden event featured a top-notch three-man field — Cunningham, Gene Venzke, and Joe Mangan. And Cunningham held the world indoor record of 4:08.4.

But it was no mistake. Mangan got off first, with Venzke and Cunningham nipping at his heels. Mangan tried to give up the lead but neither of the others wanted it. No matter how slowly he went, Venzke and Cunningham stayed right behind him.

The crowd booed loudly, but it had no effect on the runners. They reached the three-quarter-mile mark in 3:51.5, slow even by high school standards.

Venzke finally went past Mangan but failed to step up the pace. Then with less than 400 yards to go, Cunningham made his move.

Quickly he shot past his two rivals. His sudden move and fast pace caught Mangan and Venzke flat-footed. As Cunningham sprinted away, the overflow crowd changed its boos to cheers. They hadn't seen the fastest mile, but they did see one of the most unusual in history.

Weighty Affair

It seemed like an obvious mismatch. On April 30, 1900, in Brooklyn, N.Y., boxer Bob Fitzsimmons stepped into the ring weighing 172 pounds. His opponent, Ed Dunkhorst, tipped the scales at 312, 140 pounds more than Fitzsimmons.

A mismatch? Sure. But not what you'd expect. Fitzsimmons, the little man, stopped Dunkhorst in two rounds.

Shot Gun

Every golfer has bad days. But no one has come close to an unfortunate woman player who took a week's worth of shots on a single hole at Shawnee-on-Delaware, Pa.

She teed up the ball on the par-3, 130-yard 16th hole and promptly hooked it into a nearby river. When she saw the ball floating atop the water, she and her husband got into a boat and rowed after it. When she arrived at the ball, she began flailing away. She took stroke after stroke until she — and the ball — finally reached dry land, one and a half miles downstream.

Then she had to pitch the ball through heavy woods before reaching the green. Her total for the hole — 166 strokes, only 163 over par!

There's no record of whether she ever played again.